By Tayyaba Syed & Umm Nura

Vancouver

To my husband, my constant, my best friend: I pray Allah continues to shine you like a jewel from Jannah for me in this life and the next. −T.S.

To my husband, who created this dream alongside me and when I said, "What shall we call the four friends?" He said, "The Jannah Jewels." - U.N.

Published by Gentle Breeze Books, Vancouver, B.C., Canada

Copyright 2016 by Umm Nura
Illustrations by Nayzak Al-Hilali

Visit us on the Web! www.JannahJewels.com

ISBN:978-1-988337-00-5

March 2016

Contents

Sport:

Archery

Role:

Guides and leads the girls

Superpower:

Intense sight and spiritual insight

Fear:

Spiders

Special Gadget:

Ancient Compass

Carries:

Bow and Arrow, Ancient Map, Compass

Sport:

Skateboarding

Role:

Artist, Racer

Superpower:

Fast racer on foot or skateboard

Fear:

Hunger (She's always hungry!)

Special Gadget:

Time Travel Watch

Carries:

Skateboard, Sketchpad, Pencil, Watch

Sport:

Horseback Riding

Role:

Walking Encyclopedia,
Horseback Rider

Superpower:

Communicates with
animals

Fear:

Heights

Special Gadget:

Book of Knowledge

Carries:

Book of Knowledge, has
horse named "Spirit"

Sport:

Swimming

Role:

Environmentalist,
Swimmer

Superpower:

Breathes underwater for
a long time

Fear:

Drowning

Special Gadget:

Metal Ball

Carries:

Sunscreen, Water
canteen, Metal Ball

SUPPORTING CHARACTERS

JAFFAR

GENERAL HASSAN

SULTAN MUHAMMAD

THE JANNAH JEWELS ADVENTURE 7

TURKEY

ARTIFACT 7: SULTAN'S TASBIH

"God has given each of us different skills and strengths. We must learn to use them for His sake at the right time and the right place."

~ Master Runner

As salaamu alaikum Dear Readers,

So far, the Jewels have successfully found ancient manuscripts in Timbuktu, a medicinal plant from China, a scroll pen from Baghdad, two vials of mercury and sand from Spain, and an argan kernel seed from Morocco.

Now, we are so excited to bring to you the beauty and splendor of magnificent Turkey through the eyes of the amazing Jannah Jewels.

They are back with an all new action-packed adventure. They travel back in time to the Conquest of Constantinople and find themselves right in the middle of it all!

They must work together as a team to find strength and courage to get them through this intense journey. The Jewels learn to use their skills to the best of their abilities while relying on God to help them every step of the way.

New friendships are made along the way. They even meet the great conqueror, Sultan Muhammad II, who Prophet Muhammad, peace and blessings be upon him, had predicted would come as a great leader for Islam. They also learn about the wonderful Companion named Abu Ayub al-Ansari, may God be pleased with him, who hosted the Prophet in his home when he first arrived to Madinah. How blessed was he!

See what obstacles the Jannah Jewels must face to gain a Triumph in Turkey!

With warmest salaams,
Tayyaba Syed & Umm Nura

1

Obstacles

The air seemed heavy to Hidayah today. The sky was draped with thick clouds as if carrying with them a big change. She looked at her best friends Iman, Jaide and Sara sitting in front of her with the backdrop of the perfect balance of nature: high trees crowned with rich, green leaves stretching along the peaceful shore of the Pacific Ocean.

Hidayah felt grateful for having such amazing teammates. She watched as Iman had her nose in a book, Jaide sketched the sky into her sketchpad, and Sara was sifting her fingers through the sand in search of tiny seashells.

The Terra Nova Nature Park in Richmond was a sight to see. It was one of Hidayah's favorite places to hang out ever since she was little. It seemed magical: a place she could escape from her loneliness as an orphaned child. Being back at this park with the Jannah Jewels made her feel complete, like pieces of a puzzle coming together.

"What are you thinking about?" Iman asked as she walked over and nudged Hidayah's waist with her elbow.

Hidayah took a moment to speak. "Why do you think Sensei wanted to meet us here today instead of the dojo?"

Iman adjusted her glasses higher up onto the bridge of her nose. "Maybe we will find out about our next mission," she guessed. Meanwhile, Jaide and Sara came and sat next to them, dragging grains of sand along with their bare feet.

"It's too soon for that," Hidayah speculated, since the Jannah Jewels had only been back from Morocco a few days ago. "The missions seem to be getting harder each time. We will probably have to work harder as a team and do some serious training first before we are sent off again."

"Training? Here?!" Jaide questioned. "We don't even have any of our equipment with us. You didn't bring your bow and arrow, Iman didn't bring Spirit, and I don't have a skateboard anymore."

"I have my metal ball and water canteen though!" Sara chimed in enthusiastically.

"Okay, if we need a flashlight 8 hours from now or get thirsty, we can count on you," Jaide said playfully.

"Hey! That flashlight saved us out of that dark cellar back in Fes and fixed our mixed-up time-travel in Andalusia. "Don't be ungrateful," Sara reminded her.

"I'm hungry," said Jaide trying to change the subject. "I hope Sensei comes soon."

Just as Jaide mentioned her name, a gentle voice called out from behind them.

"*As salaamu alaikum.*"

The Jannah Jewels quickly stood up to greet

Sensei Elle.

"*Wa alaikum as salaam*," they all replied simultaneously. To the girls' surprise, Sensei was not alone.

"Mamá?" Sara was shocked to see her mother standing next to Sensei. Mrs. Bellamy smiled but remained silent.

"Girls, as you know, this is Sara's mother, but you will only be referring to her as 'Master Runner' while you train with her."

The Jannah Jewels stared at Mrs. Bellamy completely puzzled.

"Peace be upon you," said Mrs. Bellamy. "I'm so happy to be here."

"Master Runner is a master of the art of parkour from France, and I have asked her to come and teach you girls before the summer ends. She will be working with you all for the next month," Sensei Elle informed them.

"Wait. What?" Sara felt so lost. "Mamá? You know parkour?!"

Mrs. Bellamy simply nodded and smiled back.

"I'm so confused! How? When? Who? Why?!" Sara was flabbergasted.

Hidayah leaned into Sara's ear. "It's okay," she whispered. "Just listen."

Sara turned and looked at Hidayah with her mouth wide-open. Hidayah squeezed Sara's hand to calm her.

"Thank you, Sensei Elle, for letting me share this with the girls," said Mrs. Bellamy. "God-willing, they will learn and flourish quickly. They won't let you down."

Sensei Elle lowered her head slightly with a thin-lipped smile in response. "May Allah be with you all," she prayed and turned away from the group. Her red robes flowed behind her as she walked off the beach.

Mrs. Bellamy was wearing a full-sleeved shirt with joggers and running shoes covered in sand. She had a two-piece white *hijab* tucked in tightly into her shirt's crew collar. "Okay, are we ready?" she asked excitedly as she rubbed her hands together.

The Jannah Jewels stood speechless not knowing what to expect.

"Each day, we will build upon your skills pushing you further and further," Mrs. Bellamy informed the Jannah Jewels. "I expect each of you to be here early for practice and ready to give your all. Every time you feel like quitting or not working as hard, I want you to ask yourself one question: if you're not better than you were the day before, then what have you accomplished today?"

"Wow! That's deep," whispered Jaide to Hidayah, who nudged her to stay quiet.

"Now, eventually, our goal is to be able to run freely, not letting any obstacle stand in the way," said Mrs. Bellamy. "If you think…"

"Mamá?" Sara interrupted her mom.

Mrs. Bellamy cleared her throat.

"Umm, I mean Master Runner?" Sara hesitantly corrected herself. "How will we be able to get over these supposed 'obstacles'?"

"Like this," replied her mother, who immediately

turned and sped down the shore toward a tall pile of huge boulders.

"Mamá! Stop! What are you doing?" Sara screamed with instant fear, but there was no stopping her mother.

Mrs. Bellamy did not slow down as she reached the wall of sharp rocks. She jumped up towards them climbing up with her arms and feet as if she was a human spider. She reached the top of the highest rock and turned to wave at the Jannah Jewels.

"Whoa!" screamed Hidayah and Iman.

"Someone catch me! I'm going to faint!" Sara's legs began to buckle. Jaide caught her and pushed her back up onto her feet.

"I always knew your mom was cool," said Jaide. "But I never knew she was *this* cool!"

The girls then watched as Mrs. Bellamy jumped from the top of the rock pile down to the sandy floor.

"Noooo!" Sara shrieked falling down onto her knees.

Her mom somersaulted down tucking her head into her chest and rolling onto the beach like a ball until she was able to stand back up. Then she ran just as fast back to the girls whose jaws hung open. Mrs. Bellamy returned fully composed as if nothing had happened.

"Any questions?"

All four Jannah Jewels shot their hands up in the air.

*   *   *   *

The day was gruesome for the Jannah Jewels. Master Runner had completely changed the girls' training method. They had to do endless sprints, pull-ups, dips, squats, jumps, knee-ups, push-ups, and many other exercises they had never done before. They left the park with aching bones and burning muscles.

"I still don't understand why you never told me, Mamá," Sara said to her mother that night. She had invited the rest of the Jannah Jewels to dinner, so they could learn more about her mom's hidden talent. They each sat around the square dining table

8

with packets of ice wrapped around their arms, knees and ankles.

"It's like you are this great super athlete that I never knew about," said Sara before taking a sip of her potato soup.

Mrs. Bellamy buttered her French roll slowly as she spoke. "God has given each of us different skills and strengths. We must learn to use them for His sake at the right time and the right place."

"Okay, I get that, but why have I never seen you do parkour before?" Sara asked. "Do you have any idea how cool you are?"

Her mother giggled softly. "Oh, so I wasn't cool before, eh?"

"You know what I mean," said Sara. "I wish you had been training me since I was little."

"And us!" Jaide chimed in as she stuffed chunks of potatoes into her mouth.

"Parkour is learning to use your body for what it's made for: movement," Mrs. Bellamy spoke between bites of her homemade bread. "It embodies the values of honesty, respect, humility, sacrifice and hard work. Sensei Elle told me you and your friends are improving on all these aspects and thinks you are ready to learn this great art form of selflessness," she said.

"Art form?" Hidayah questioned as she massaged her sore legs.

"Yes, first, you must learn how to face your fears and then reapply this to your life. When you put your fears aside and trust in Allah, doors open and you can face anything. You must be able to control your mind and heart in order to master the art of parkour," answered Mrs. Bellamy.

Hidayah thought about how similar parkour was to the art of archery. Sensei had taught her to unite her mind with her heart and how one must release her fears before she releases an arrow.

"Parkour gives one the ability to overcome any potential obstacles, be it physical or mental," said Mrs. Bellamy. "It makes you realize the only limitations you have are the ones you set for yourself. Today's training was just a sampling of what's to come. Be ready. It's going to get much more intense," she warned.

The Jannah Jewels all moaned in protest.

And she was not kidding. Every day that month, the Jannah Jewels trained hard with Master Runner. Terra Nova was the perfect nature-made obstacle course in Vancouver full of tall trees for climbing, giant rocks for leaping and jumping, and an open shore to run as freely as possible. Master Runner pushed the girls each day to work harder, run faster, climb higher, and jump farther. They would not compete against each other, but instead, work as a team and support one another's strengths and abilities.

"Are you ready?" Master Runner asked the Jannah Jewels as they lined up to charge towards the same pile of boulders Mrs. Bellamy had climbed the first day of training.

Everyone seemed ready except for Iman who had been working extra hard to conquer her fear of heights. She quickly calmed her nerves by sending prayers upon the Prophet Muhammad, peace and blessings be upon him.

"Yes!" the others shouted, focusing on the great obstacle ahead of them. After a slight delay, Iman had gathered herself together and then nodded to Master Runner.

"On your marks, get set, *Bismillah*!" shouted Master Runner.

The Jewels dashed as fast as they could towards the rocks. Tracks of shoe prints lay in the sand behind them.

"Go, Jewels, go! You can do it!" cheered Mrs. Bellamy.

One-by-one, the girls leaped onto the rock pile climbing higher and higher up. Hidayah could feel beads of sweat dripping from inside her *hijab* down her face. Her arms burned with pain as she reached higher and tried to hold on with all her might. From her peripheral vision, she could see the other Jewels climbing up the sides of the jagged walls alongside her including Iman.

"Please God, You are the Most High. Give us strength and remove our fears," she prayed. She climbed up and up and before she knew it, she

had reached the top and crawled up to a standing position above the giant stone wall. Iman, Jaide and Sara crawled up beside her. They stood up shouting with joy and amazement. Iman was shaking with disbelief. They waved at Master Runner, who raced towards them with delight.

"Praise be to God! You all did it!" she congratulated them from below.

The view from atop was surreal. Hidayah could see for miles down the vast shore, which was decorated with rows of towering trees and strands of clouds in the distance. She should have felt overjoyed at this amazing moment like her friends who were hugging and high-fiving each other with happiness. However, a strange realization came over her at that moment.

As she stood high above the ground, her heart fell down to her stomach. *What type of obstacle will we have to face on our next mission?* Hidayah wondered with worry.

2

Recovery

Worry was all Jasmin knew for the last month. Her eyes were bloodshot and sleep-deprived. Her back was sore from sitting in the cheap leather chair all night, and her left arm itched severely under the brace. She tried to readjust herself to a semi-comfortable position but to no avail.

The compact, white-walled room smelled like disinfectants and rubbing alcohol. She stared hard at her father's face as she replaced the wet cloth on his head with a fresh one. She pressed it gently, examining his creases and wrinkles behind the shadows of his salt-and-pepper colored beard closely. There was pain, tension, frustration, struggles… life written all over his sleeping long, boney face. She noticed the white hairs had overtaken the black ones in his beard.

She felt the side of his head. It was still hot. The fever kept fluctuating, but Khan had not fully awoken yet. He would have random outbursts in his unconsciousness calling out his wife Layla's name, but nobody else. A tear fell from Jasmin's cheek onto the tip of Khan's nose. He laid still.

This last month had been an emotional roller coaster for Jasmin. She felt so many different things in her heart, sometimes all at once, yet had no one to talk to. The one feeling that overpowered her most was anger. She was mad at the Jannah Jewels, especially Sara for knocking Khan off his feet and causing his grade three concussion. The hospital scans showed there was no permanent brain damage but the swelling was still there, which meant he may have some side effects once conscience again. It would take time and care to heal the doctors had told her.

As his body was working hard at recovering, it kept breaking out into a fever every few days.

Jasmin alone was constantly nursing him. She would dedicate morning and night to serving her father. She felt empty. She felt alone. She felt sadness. A small part of her missed her mother. Should she inform her mother of this injury? *No! She does not deserve to know. She was the one who left them,* Jasmin remembered. Then all her emotions turned into anger once again.

Why isn't Jaffar here? Why hasn't he come to check up on Father? Doesn't he care? This is all his doing anyway. Father was going after Jaffar before his awful fall. If only he had stayed out of Father's way. If only he didn't go against Father's wishes. How dare he try to help the Jannah Jewels?

Jasmin's mind raced with fury. She despised her brother and her mother, who had now both walked out on her. Even more so, though, Jasmin detested the Jannah Jewels for all the problems they had caused.

She looked down at her father and wanted nothing more than to have him wake up from this vegetable state.

"Oh, Father. Please wake up. I need you," she cried squeezing his hand tightly against her wet cheek. She felt his cold hand grip hers back. She lifted her head in disbelief. "Father! Father! It's me! Jasmin!"

"Laylaaaaaa," Khan moaned, his eyes still shut.

A feeling of irritation and frustration came over Jasmin. *Why was he remembering the woman that left him and his children? Why was he calling out to Layla when it was Jasmin sitting by his side day and night?*

Putting her annoyed state aside, Jasmin slowly removed the cloth from her father's head. Beads of sweat had formed across his wrinkled forehead. His skin seemed cooler as she dried off the sweat.

Jasmin became startled from a sudden knock at the door. "Who is it?" she asked as she wiped the thick tears from her eyes. She stood up and walked over to the entrance of the hospital room. There was another loud knock at the door. She opened the door and froze. It was her Uncle Idrees looking a bit worried and slightly distracted.

"What are *you* doing here?" Jasmin asked with annoyance.

Uncle Idrees now focused all his attention on his niece. "Is that how you greet your uncle?"

Jasmin rolled her eyes as she reluctantly mumbled *'salaam'* under her breath.

He narrowed his eyes with displeasure and then took a nervous look around the hospital corridor. "May I come in?" he asked after a few odd moments.

"Why? What's the point? You haven't come to see your brother in a month. Why now?" There was clear resentment in Jasmin's voice.

"I see that you have lost your manners," Uncle Idrees said in a monotone fashion. "How do you know that I haven't come before? You're never here when I visit."

Jasmin took a step back in disbelief. *How could that be?* she thought. She was with her father majority of the day and night. "What are you talking about? I'm always here with Father!"

Uncle Idrees gave Jasmin a slight smile.

19

"Except when you briefly go home to freshen up," he responded, his eyes still searching awkwardly around the entrance of the room.

Jasmin's heartbeat sped up with anger again. Her face became red and hot as her eyes pierced at her uncle. "You are up to something again just like you were in the bazaar with Jaffar! I don't believe you! I don't want you here! Now leave!"

"Laylaaaa," Khan stirred restlessly with his eyes closed.

Uncle Idrees peered over Jasmin's head at his brother, who lay still on the bed. "I must see him now, Jasmin," Uncle Idrees protested. "Let me in, child! You mustn't interfere in adult matters. His condition is serious, and I must be with him. He is my little brother before he is your father!" He stared at her firmly, keeping his stout posture stiff.

Tears began to flow from Jasmin's gray eyes uncontrollably. Her shoulders fell as she placed her wet face into her hands. "I don't like any of you," she sobbed. "All of you did this to him: you, Jaffar, Mother, the Jannah Jewels! No one cares about him except for me, yet he only asks for Mother! He was the only one that loved me, and now he has forgotten about me too!" She let out loud piercing cries that hiccupped with pain and disappointment.

Uncle Idrees walked up to his niece and wrapped his arm around her shoulders. She continued crying with her face in his chest.

"Jasmin, don't think like this," he held onto the back of her head as she soaked his robe with her tears. "How can you be forgotten? You are loved by all of us including both your parents, brother *and* me."

She looked up at him as she sniffed back her runny nose and wiped her tears off her cheeks. He handed her a handkerchief from his pocket. His eyes were black just like her father's.

"You are a mess," her uncle said, as he looked her up and down with concern. "Come back to my place to get a good meal and some proper rest. Let me sit with Khan for a few minutes, and then I'll take you back with me. Your aunt will be happy to see you. It's been a while since she has laid her eyes on your beautiful face."

Jasmin clumsily adjusted her *hijab* and gave her uncle a faint smile.

He sat her down in the hospital chair and went and stood next to his brother's bed side. He placed his right hand on Khan's forehead and recited some silent prayers. After a few minutes, he leaned over and kissed his brother's head. "Allah hears you," he whispered into Khan's ear. Khan did not move.

Uncle Idrees then turned and looked at Jasmin. Her mood had completely changed. She was calm and content.

"Shall we?" he asked her with a welcoming grin.

Jasmin nodded and grabbed her things. "Will he be okay?" Jasmin asked with worry in her voice.

"Yes, *in sha Allah*, God-willing."

They both looked back at the frozen figure lying there. Uncle Idrees fixed his small rimless hat on his round head as he escorted Jasmin out of the hospital room. She hesitated leaving her father for the night but felt a sense of trust from her uncle.

As they quickly walked out of the hospital, Jasmin noticed his vision wandering in a strange manner.

"Are you looking for someone?"

Uncle Idrees turned his attention back to Jasmin.

"We are going the right way, correct?"

Jasmin stared at her uncle in a very puzzled way. "I thought you have been here before," she said.

"Yes, yes. It's been a long day. Come along now," he pulled her hurriedly behind him.

That was the first night in a long time that Jasmin slept peacefully. Her aunt and uncle made her feel welcome and at ease. As the morning sun seeped through the long, thin curtains, Jasmin awoke with a renewed sense of hope. She quickly changed and ran downstairs anticipating a nice breakfast with her relatives. She was surprised to find no one home.

Jasmin entered the kitchen and found a warm plate of eggs and fresh-baked bread with a hand-written note placed next to it.

Dear Jasmin,

Sorry, we had to step out early this morning.

Please enjoy some breakfast before you head out. You are welcome to come by any time. Our doors are always open for you.

Love,

Uncle Idrees & Aunt Nur

A sudden feeling of loneliness came over Jasmin. She was not expecting to be greeted by a note this morning. She wanted nothing more than to get back to her father. She took a few bites of her breakfast and headed straight to the hospital.

As Jasmin walked over to the building, she wondered how her father's condition would be today. There had not been much improvement in his health over the last month. She entered his room thinking she will again find her father lying still and unconscious in bed. Instead, she herself became motionless when she saw him. Khan was sitting up in his bed, awake with a lost look on his face.

"Father! You're better!" Jasmin ran to Khan overwhelmed with happiness and wrapped her good arm around his shoulders. Her body shook as she cried more than she had the entire month.

Khan pulled her gently away from him. "Who are you?"

Jasmin looked at her father in shock.

"Father. I'm Jasmin. Your daughter," she said with tears still trickling down her face.

"Ahhh!" Khan suddenly gasped in pain squeezing his head between his hands.

"Father! What's wrong?"

"Please leave me alone!" Khan demanded. He then looked up at his daughter with confusion in his eyes. "I don't know who you are!"

Jasmin felt as if her entire world had come to an end. She slowly walked backwards away from her father who looked at her like a stranger. She dragged her feet out of the hospital room closing the door behind her. Her heart ached and burned at the same time. She could not breathe. She could not think. *How could this be? How could Father forget me? What am I going to do?*

Blood raced through her throbbing veins. Her breaths became fast and deep. She pulled the brace off her healing arm and tossed it forcefully down to the white-tiled floor. She was done trying to recover.

"I will make the Jannah Jewels pay for this!" she vowed to herself.

3

Surprises

Sara vowed to get over this. More than a month had passed since the Jannah Jewels had been back from Morocco, and Sara continuously had a nightmare every night. She would wake up sweaty and frightened in a flutter of panic. Someone was chasing her and getting closer each time. Sitting upright on her bed, she would recite a prayer seeking refuge in God like Prophet Muhammad, peace and blessings be upon him, had advised to do after a bad dream. She would then make *wudhu*, offer prayers to her Lord at whatever time of night it was, and then stay up until the dawn prayer reading the *Holy Qur'an* and doing *dhikr*. Then she would head up the hill to Sensei Elle's dojo to pray *Fajr* with the other Jannah Jewels.

She would arrive to the dojo every morning sleep-deprived and on edge. Sara did not know how to even begin telling her friends about these awful dreams. She had been strong and brave in Fes against Khan and helped save Jaide, Mus'ab and herself from him and his men. Ever since their return, though, she kept having flashbacks of the skateboard crash, the chase, the kidnapping, waking up in the dark cellar, the scary encounter with Khan and Jasmin, and being attacked by shooting arrows. They managed to escape thanks to God's help. Throughout their mission, they had constantly called on Him for help and guidance, and He had protected them through it all.

Sara was looking forward to finally getting her mind off of things today. She was actually excited about Jaide's party and knew it would be an awesome celebration. After the intense training Master Runner had put the Jewels through the last few weeks, plus the lack of proper sleep, Sara was ready for a change of pace. This would be the perfect escape from it all.

She quickly changed into a loose high-low floral

dress with solid white leggings underneath and a white cardigan on top. She stood in front of her full-length mirror and made a prayer for God to beautify her inside and out. Sara then adorned the outfit with a matching peach-colored headscarf fastening it with a jeweled pin and slipped on a set of silver bangles on each hand.

"Sara, hon! You are running late! Come down already!" her mother called from downstairs.

"I'll be right there," she responded. She took once last look at herself and took a deep breath. "It's only a dream. There is no power nor might except from God. Oh God, ease my heart and remove my worries," she prayed.

She took out her metal ball from the backpack on her bed and placed it into a small, cross-body purse, which she then slipped on over her neck and shoulder. Sara quickly grabbed her gift bag for Jaide and swiftly ran down the stairs.

"I'm here, Mamá. I'll be back in a couple hours *in sha Allah*, God-willing."

"Okay, call me when you get there and before

you leave," her mother directed her.

Sara nodded, hugged her mother and said *salaam*. She went out from the garage, slid her helmet carefully onto her head making sure not to mess up her *hijab*, and lifted her dress as she got onto her bike. She recited the traveling *du'a* and then rode down her driveway.

The Jannah Jewels all lived on the same street. As she rolled down the block, she rode past Hidayah's house lined with green siding first. Her aunt was kneeling on the front lawn mending her beautiful garden.

"*As salaamu alaikum, Aunt Khadija!*" Sara greeted in transit.

"*Wa alaikum as salaam*, Sara," Hidayah's aunt waved back.

A few minutes later, she came up to Iman's white stucco home but no one seemed to be home.

I better hurry, thought Sara.

She pulled up to Jaide's red brick home marked with a colorful bunch of balloons tied to its mailbox.

Sara parked her bike next to Hidayah and Iman's and entered through the open garage.

Sara was welcomed by the aroma of baked sweets and pizza. She placed her gift on the dining table and called her mom from the kitchen's phone. She then followed the collective sound of her friends giggling and screaming and found them playing tag in Jaide's backyard.

"There you are!" said Jaide as Sara stepped onto the back deck.

"Wouldn't miss it," Sara reassured her. "You look great, Jaide!"

Jaide was wearing a long, purple Chinese dress. She ran up and whacked Sara on the hand and invited her into the game. "You're it!" she told Sara.

"Hey!" Sara said laughingly as she chased after her friends.

After games, fun crafts, a warm lunch, and tasty desserts, the girls all crowded around Jaide in the living room ready to give her the gift. Sara handed Jaide the gift bag she had brought.

"This is from Hidayah, Iman and me," she told her. "We are so proud of you for memorizing *Surah Yaseen*."

Jaide smiled shyly and removed the tissue from the bag. She pulled out a new sketchpad with a pretty purple ribbon tied around it. On the cover it read, '*To our favorite Jannah Jewel.*'

"Wow, this is beautiful!" she said as she untied the ribbon.

"We noticed yours was getting pretty full, and we still have a few more missions to go," Hidayah explained.

"I love it," Jaide told them hugging the sketchpad against her chest. "Umm Amin really inspired me on the last mission. When she told us that she had memorized the entire *Qur'an*, I prayed for Allah to give me the same honor one day. I came back determined to finish memorizing *Yaseen*."

"Make *du'a* for us too please," said Hidayah.

Just then Mrs. Yin walked into the room holding a long, large wrapped box.

"This is from us," she told Jaide. "Your father and I are so pleased with your *Qur'anic* efforts," said her mother.

Jaide gazed with wonderment at the giant present and enthusiastically took it from her mother. The Jannah Jewels all watched anxiously as she quickly tore open the gift.

There was a loud pain-staking screech in the air. Jaide was screaming with surprise.

"Oh mi gosh! I can't believe it! No way! Is this really the Thunderbolt 1000 electric skateboard?!" she asked her mom in shock.

Mrs. Yin gave a big smile as her eyes sparkled proudly.

The girls all jumped up and down with excitement. They delightfully examined the black long sleek skateboard with its bright neon yellow wheels.

"Look, they even got it engraved for you," pointed Iman to the back of skateboard. There was a yellow lightning bolt with Jaide's name running across its center.

"This is just awesome, Mom!" said Jaide squeezing her mother tight. She then turned to the other Jannah Jewels. "Let's go try it out. We can ride up to the dojo!"

"I charged it last night," Mrs. Yin informed them. "Go have fun and be safe. Don't forget your helmet!"

"Yesssss!" the girls all hissed together.

Sara had forgotten all about her fears. She was so happy for Jaide and loving every minute together with her friends. Jaide hurriedly raced up the hill on her new board as the other Jewels rode their bikes behind her. It was hard for them to keep up with the electric board's speed.

"Woo hoo!" screamed Jaide with the wind in her face and the sun behind her. They pulled up to the dojo anticipating Sensei Elle's reaction. The new skateboard would be a great addition to their next mission.

They ran around the ins and outs of the dojo in search of Sensei, but they could not find her anywhere. They came upon the other Masters huddled together in a serious conversation reading a piece of paper. When they saw the Jannah Jewels approach them, they immediately stopped talking.

"*As salaamu alaikum*," the girls greeted them.

"*Wa alaikum as salaam*," the Masters replied one-by-one with concerned faces.

"Do you know where Sensei Elle is?" asked Hidayah.

The Masters nervously looked at one another. They remained quiet for what seemed like forever.

The Master Rider finally spoke up. "We are not sure," she told them hesitantly. "She seems to be... missing."

The Jannah Jewels stared at the Masters, their eyes bulging with disbelief. In that moment, Sara felt all her worries suddenly rush back to her.

4

Mission Impossible

"Did she leave in a rush? What happened? Where did she go?" Hidayah fretfully fired questions at the Masters. She felt her heart was going to burst out of her chest.

"We were just going to call you four," Master Swimmer replied. "We have no information except for this poem she left for you," she said holding a paper in her hand.

"May we see it?" asked Hidayah.

Master Swimmer handed over the paper. The Jewels all huddled around as Hidayah read the poem aloud:

"The time is here.

You must leave all your fears.

Take only that which you need.

Great strength comes from your creed.

The Opener you shall meet,

A leader praised by the Elite.

Recognize the one behind the fire,

For courage you will acquire.

Many obstacles will come your way,

Near the Host you must pray.

Climb high, climb fast

For there will be a great blast.

A string of remembrance you shall find.

A father's memory remains behind."

"What in the world?!" Jaide stared at her friends in total disarray.

"What does all this mean?" asked Hidayah to the four Masters.

"We assume she wants you to go on your next

mission," Master Rider answered with hesitation.

"And where is that?" asked Iman.

Silence came over the gathering.

"Unfortunately, we do not know," spoke Master Artist. "We pray God paints a clear picture for you all."

"*Ameen*," responded the other Masters together.

"How can we go like this?" Jaide protested. "We're wearing dresses!"

"*I* always get by in a skirt," Iman reminded her. "Sensei said to only take what we need. You have your time-traveling watch and new board, I have my *Book of Knowledge*, and Sara has her metal ball."

"But I didn't bring my bow and arrow or the ancient map," Hidayah noted worriedly.

"I think this is why she wanted us to learn parkour and left us this note," Iman guessed. "All we need is ourselves and God."

Hidayah sighed deeply. *This mission seems impossible*, she thought to herself. *How will we locate the ancient artifact without the map? How will we face danger without any equipment?*

She knew she could not voice her concerns to the other Jewels. She had to be strong and positive for their sake. She remembered the words from the *Holy Qu'ran* that Sensei had taught them: *God suffices us and what a great Guardian is He.* She realized this would be the first time they left for a mission without seeing Sensei.

"What about Sensei?" she asked the Masters. "How will we find her?"

The Masters exchanged uneasy glances at one another.

"We will do what we can from here," said Master Swimmer. "You all focus on the task at hand and work as a team. Now go down to the time-travelling maple tree and leave at once. God is your Witness," she told them.

Hidayah folded the poem and handed it to Sara. "I've got no pockets or backpack with me," said Hidayah. "Can you stick this into your purse?"

"Sure," Sara answered doing just that.

"Let's go!" Hidayah said as she led the girls down the hill to their favorite maple tree in the neighborhood park. The Jannah Jewels ran as fast as they could behind her.

"Ready?" Hidayah asked as she caught her breath.

Iman, Jaide and Sara nodded.

Hidayah noticed the anxiety on each of their faces. "Remember, we are a team. We will get through this mission, because we know God is our Guardian," she reassured her friends.

With heavy, nervous hearts and sweaty palms, they pushed the trunk of the maple tree and slid down, down, down to the bottom of a tunnel. They each stood up, dusted themselves off and then locked hands forming a tight circle together. All four Jannah Jewels closed their eyes and recited together, "*Bismillah hir Rahman nir Raheem.*"

5

Darkness

Hidayah opened her eyes and looked up at the waning moon. Its light was the only thing shining the way for the Jannah Jewels. They were standing under a tall Eastern plane tree with an enormously wide trunk, its leaves creating shadows on the ground from the moonlight. The sound of the crickets chirping and a slight whistle of the wind were all that the girls could hear. The grass smelled fresh, and the air had a clean and pleasant scent carrying a cool breeze with it.

Sara felt calmness here. She reached into her pouch slung by a rope across her body and pulled out her metal ball. She tapped it hard to light it up. She lifted the ball above her head and moved it around to find something recognizable or familiar in their surroundings. They had landed in a dark forest full of centennial trees with no one in sight.

"Where are we?" Iman asked tensely.

"Looks like we are in the middle of a forest," Hidayah stated.

"More like middle of nowhere," added Jaide.

"And it looks like the middle of the night too," Iman noted adjusting her glasses in hopes of seeing better in the dark. "Sara, lower the light away from our eyes. It will take our eyes 20 to 30 minutes to adapt to the dark."

"How will we see then?" questioned Sara.

"You'll see," Iman responded. "God created our eyes so well."

Following Iman's suggestion, Sara shined the ball of light towards the grass. She saw Hidayah sitting on the ground in deep thought, the bottom of her dress forming a perfect circle around her.

"What's wrong?" she asked her.

"My heart feels heavy here," answered Hidayah.

"Like a good heavy. There's something really special about this place."

Sara and the others joined Hidayah on the grass.

"What do you think it is?" asked Jaide.

"I don't know yet," said Hidayah. She looked back up at the sky. "What I do know is that we need to pray. It's *Tahajjud* time, a time of accepted prayer. We have never been so lost like this before. We need to ask God for help."

"Jaide should lead the prayer of need," Sara suggested.

Jaide's eyes grew big. "What?! Me?!"

"Yes, I agree," Hidayah said. "Remember what Sensei taught us: *in the heart of the night, with the heart of the Qur'an, from the heart of the believer, ask Allah for what you need. Tahajjud* time is the heart of the night, and *Surah Yaseen* is the heart of the *Qur'an*. It's the perfect formula, which *you* can do now, Jaide," Hidayah encouraged her, making eye contact with her in the faint light they had.

Jaide then immediately stood up. "Okay."

Sara, who was very aware of the environment, carefully studied the stars above. "The *Qibla* is that way," she said pointing east.

The girls lined up on the sides of Jaide. They each took a deep breath as they began the prayer. The verses of the 36th chapter of the *Holy Book* flowed freely from Jaide's heart, the words and her voice bringing comfort to the congregation. When she reached the verse, "*Peace is the word from the Merciful Lord,*" she felt at ease. She realized that was what the Jannah Jewels were working towards: gaining God's Peace. Once the prayer was completed, the Jewels remained seated and each made quiet supplications from their hearts for help on this mission.

Suddenly, they heard heavy footsteps marching rapidly towards them.

"Sara, get rid of the light!" Hidayah ordered.

Sara fumbled to reach for her metal ball as the footsteps drew closer and closer. She quickly turned it off and slipped it back into her pouch.

"Quick! Hide!" whispered Iman.

The girls all scrambled to their feet, stumbling in their party dresses trying to find a safe hiding spot.

"This way!" Hidayah signaled pulling the girls behind the gigantic trunk of the tall tree where they had originally arrived. "Shhh," she quieted them. All four Jewels formed a tight cluster together, their hearts racing with fear.

"Who's there?" a man called out in a deep voice nearby. The girls could see a faint glow from what looked like a torch flame.

The Jannah Jewels became cold as each of them wondered the same thing at that moment: *How were they going to escape?* Their hearts drummed quick, heavy beats as their eyes wandered to and fro in the darkness. They hugged the tree trunk hard being careful not to make a sound.

Hidayah then felt something crawling up her arm inside her dress.

Spider! she thought to herself. The thought of a spider crawling on her seemed scarier than being captured by a stranger. She shook her arm forcefully in an effort to ward off the creepy, crawly creature.

In doing so, the seeds from the keepsake bracelet Umm Amin gave her on their last mission clattered together loudly.

All of a sudden, the man grabbed her arm and yanked her out from behind the tree.

"There you are!" shouted a tall, long-haired bearded man wearing a pointed helmet and a long full-sleeved shirt under a leather armor suit. He looked like a soldier with a sword hung from his waist, his face lit from the torch in his hand.

Hidayah and the Jewels were completely frightened.

"Who are you?!" he questioned shining the flame at Iman, Jaide, and Sara.

The girls were trapped.

Oh God, what do we do? Hidayah quickly made a prayer in her heart. *God, You are the Protector and the Helper. Please protect us and help us.*

Just then, Jaide remembered the verse she had recited from *Surah Yaseen* shortly before: *Peace is the word from the Merciful Lord.*

"May God's Peace be upon you," Jaide's voice trembled as she greeted the fearsome stranger.

The man's eyes suddenly softened. He released his grip from Hidayah's arm.

"*Wa alaikum as salaam*," he spoke calmly now. "Why are you girls wandering here alone at night? How did you end up here?"

Hidayah gathered the nerve to speak up. She figured this man must be guarding something important. "This place is special. We wanted to visit it."

"The Sultan would not approve of this. You are trespassing," he said.

"Take us to him. We would like to meet him actually," Hidayah replied boldly.

The man became surprised at her request. "He's not going to meet children in the midst of a siege! Besides, there are no females allowed here!" the man answered, his tone getting loud.

"You must take us to him," pleaded Hidayah. "He has something we need."

"Yes, we have nothing to do with the siege," added Iman. "We just need to meet with him, and then we will be on our way."

The soldier stared hard at the Jannah Jewels. With grave seriousness he then said, "I will take you to Sir Ilyas. He will know what to do with you. Come with me."

Not knowing what else to do, the four Jewels cooperatively began to walk behind him. They marched silently over the grass and through the trees until they came to a wide, open arena full of countless tents of various sizes lined in an organized fashion. It was a make-shift campsite glowing with torches and small campfires that were heating iron pots and kettles.

Hidayah stood second behind Iman. She leaned in close to her ear and whispered, "Iman, you need to somehow take a look at your *Book of Knowledge*, so we can figure out where we are and in which era of time we have arrived."

Iman nodded. In a discreet manner, she removed her glasses and slipped them into her satchel.

"Excuse me, Sir," she addressed the soldier in front of her. He turned back to look at her. "Can I have a minute to go back and search for my spectacles?"

The man's face turned red and uneasy. "You mustn't be long," he said firmly. "Take this torch with you. We will wait here behind these trees. Now go quickly!"

"Yes, Sir," Iman replied.

Iman gave the other Jewels a look of reassurance. She then ran back as if to retrace her steps in search of her glasses. Once she was out of the soldier's view, she quickly hid behind a tree and pulled out the *Book of Knowledge* from her satchel. She sifted through the index in the back of the book looking for any clues about their whereabouts. She searched the word '*sultan*' which led her to a page with a photo of a man on horseback wearing a red cloak and a pointed helmet in the center of a large army. Some of the soldiers resembled the one who had found the Jewels. Iman quickly read the passage under the portrait:

"Son of the Ottoman emperor Sultan Murad II

and his wife Huma Hatun, Muhammad II was born on March 29, 1432. His father appointed him as a ruler of a province at the young age of 12 to learn the art of governance. He then took the throne after his father's death when he was only 20 years old in 1451. From a young age, Muhammad's teacher Emir Aaq Shemsuddin helped him memorize the entire Qu'ran *and taught him many subjects such as the Prophetic narrations, Islamic law, mathematics, engineering, architecture, literature, fine arts, and astronomy. Muhammad was fluent in seven languages. He was a great statesman and military leader as well as a just ruler. With his army of over 100,000 soldiers, Muhammad sieged the city of Constantinople in April of 1453..."*

"Hey! Where are you?"

Iman's heart jumped when she heard the soldier call out to her.

"Be right there!" she responded as she slipped her glasses back on her face and hid her book back into her satchel. She hurried back to the others. "Thank you again," Iman said politely to the soldier.

He gave her a suspicious look. "Let's go," he said in a stern tone.

Whiteness started to seep over the horizon now as dawn was approaching. The Jannah Jewels stayed close together behind the solidier. Iman turned to give Hidayah a nod and smile as if silently saying '*it's okay*.' Seeing Iman's confidence at that instance gave Hidayah a sense of hope.

They approached a small tent that was not too far from the forest. The soldier scanned the area to make sure no one was around.

"Sir Ilyas, are you in there?" he whispered through the fabric wall of the tent.

The girls heard some rustling from inside the tent.

"Just a minute," a soft voice called out.

A few moments later, a young, slender light-skinned man stepped out from the tent. He had a long, delicate face with bright blue eyes, his hair tied back in a wrap wearing a jacket armor and long boots.

"*Salaam*, General Hassan," he greeted the soldier. His eyes then fell upon the four girls who stood out like sore thumbs.

"*Salaam*, Sir Ilyas," General Hassan responded. "I need to take these girls to the Sultan, but they can't meet him dressed like this. I need you to help them."

"How did they get here? They are not from amongst our people nor did anyone bring children with them," Sir Ilyas whispered to General Hassan as he glared at the Jewels suspiciously.

"We are the same age as your Sultan when he first became a ruler," Iman spoke up gallantly. "Would you have dared to refer to him as a mere 'child' back then?" She had a look of defiance in her eyes. Hidayah, Jaide, and Sara cleared their throats.

General Hassan and Sir Ilyas looked dumbfounded. Iman's boldness had left them both speechless.

Sir Ilyas gave a smile of acceptance. "Please, come in," he welcomed the girls into his tent. He then nodded to General Hassan. "I will bring them to you after the morning prayer."

The girls all remained frozen in place, no one moved a muscle.

"I see why you are hesitating," he said to the Jewels. "Don't be afraid. I am one of you."

"One of us?" Hidayah questioned.

"Yes," he whispered lowering himself to the height of the girls to make better eye contact with them. He looked around to make sure no one else was listening. "My name is Ara. I'm a girl just like you."

6

Playing with Fire

The girls stared at Ara in disbelief.

"Really?" Jaide questioned her.

Her eyes sparkled as she nodded with a warm smile. "Now come in quickly before someone sees you." She lifted the curtain to let them enter her tent. The Jannah Jewels walked in one after the other.

"I will wait by my tent after prayer," General Hassan told Ara.

"Don't worry. I'll take care of them," she said.

The floor of the tent was lined with thick carpets covered in papers and scrolls full of engineering designs. There were a few cushions and sheets with a thin mattress placed in a corner. A small oil lantern glowed in the darkness next to a prayer rug. The Jewels looked around the simple tent nervously not knowing what to expect.

"Please tell me your names," Ara spoke gently as she sat down gesturing the girls to do the same.

"My name is Hidayah, and these are my friends Iman, Jaide, and Sara," she said pointing to each. "We are the Jannah Jewels, and we were sent here to find an ancient artifact that will help restore peace on Earth."

Ara carefully scanned each of the girls' faces. "I see," she replied calmly. "And what is this ancient artifact?"

"We don't know yet," said Hidayah. "That's what we need to find out."

"Well, I am truly impressed at your bravery, especially Iman's," she told them. "Going to meet the Sultan in his pavilion will not be easy, but I will do what I can to help you. We must change your attire, so you all fit in. We cannot have any girls here."

"How did you end up here then?" asked Iman.

Ara gave a clever smile. "My father and I designed the great cannon for the conquest. I am a master at molding cannons as much as him. He taught me everything he knows. I needed to be here to fire the cannon with him," she told them.

Sara let out a loud gasp. "You're *the one behind the fire!*" Sara said proudly as she remembered a line from Sensei's poem. "We are so happy to meet you!"

Hidayah, Iman and Jaide all smiled with satisfaction.

Ara let out a faint laugh. "I guess you can call me that," she said. "It's not easy being in a war, though. You must be strong and carry great courage. The Sultan has ordered today to be a day of prayer and rest. You came at just the right time. His commander-in-chief, General Hassan, will take you to him. My advice is just get what you need, and then get out fast."

The Jannah Jewels listened attentively.

"I will gather up some garments and helmets for your disguises from the equipment tent. You mustn't let anyone know who you are or your true identity," she warned them. "Wait here quietly while I go retrieve those items for you."

She carefully walked out of the tent, letting some of the dawn's early light spill into the tent. Sara pulled out the folded poem from her pouch.

"Can you believe it?" she said to her friends. "We are one step closer to finding the artifact!"

"Yes, but what about the rest of the poem?" asked Hidayah. "There's still so much we need to make out of Sensei's words. She grabbed the paper from Sara and looked at it again. Jaide and Iman leaned their heads over each of Hidayah's shoulders to quietly read the poem along with her:

The time is here.

You must leave all your fears.

Take only that which you need.

Great strength comes from your creed.

The Opener you shall meet,

A leader praised by the Elite.

Recognize the one behind the fire,

For courage you will acquire.

Many obstacles will come your way,

Near the Host you must pray.

Climb high, climb fast

For there will be a great blast.

A string of remembrance you shall find.

A father's memory remains behind.

"Who is the Opener, and who is the Elite?" Jaide asked.

"Let me check the *Book of Knowledge,*" said Iman. "Maybe those two titles are in here." She pulled out the book from her satchel and searched the index again. Neither word was in there. "Nothing," she informed them with disappointment.

"What were you able to find out earlier?" Hidayah asked Iman.

Iman turned back to the page with the Sultan's portrait. She read the same passage aloud to the others. After sharing the portion she had already read earlier, Iman stated, "This is where I had to stop reading, because General Hassan called me: *He was a great statesman and military leader as well as a just ruler. With his army of over 100,000 soldiers, Muhammad sieged the city of Constantinople in April of 1453. He hired a Hungarian engineer named Orban to create state-of-the-art weapons, which included a 27 foot long cannon that could hurl a 1300 pound projectile over a mile. The siege lasted for 53 days, and the Ottoman red standard was raised over Constantinople on May 29, 1453."*

"Wow! Ara helped make *that* giant cannon?" asked Jaide.

"Looks like it," answered Iman. "I think that's what's going to cause the '*great blast.*'"

Sara's expression quickly changed. "We have to get out of here then!" she shouted. "We can't be here when that cannon is fired!" Her eyes landed on each of her friends' faces in desperation. "Please, let's go back now," she begged.

"How are we going to leave without the artifact, Sara?" Hidayah questioned. "What if Jasmin comes here and gets it instead of us? How will we face Sensei? What will happen to the Golden Clock without the seventh artifact? Plus, we don't even know how to get back to the forest or which tree we came from. We have to put our fears aside and work as a team."

The mention of Jasmin's name put Sara in more of a panic. "You and Iman don't know what Jaide and I went through in Morocco! I've had nightmares ever since we've been back! I won't be able to handle anymore scares!" She was panting with fear.

Jaide moved in closer to Sara and placed her hand on her knee. "You're not alone, Sara," she said to her. "We are all in this together. Sensei said to leave all our fears and that great strength comes from our creed. With God's help, we will get through this just like our previous missions," Jaide tried to comfort her. Jaide glanced down at her wrist to check her time-travelling watch. She lifted its top flap to see how much time they had left on their mission.

"Uh oh!" she said suddenly.

Sara's face was hit with extreme worry again. "What's wrong?" she quickly asked.

"My watch! It's not working!" Jaide shrieked

showing the girls the watch's blank face.

"What does that mean?! Are we stuck here?" Sara questioned dreading the thought.

"Let's not panic," Hidayah intervened, although she kept thinking how much more difficult the mission will be without Jaide's watch. "I'm sure there's a logical explanation here."

"Maybe the battery is dead?" guessed Iman.

"Or maybe we are stuck in the past!" Sara said panting heavily. Before she could freak out anymore, Ara slipped back into the tent.

"Look, ladies! I found enough garments and armor to transform you into fierce warriors," she said laughingly. She looked up at the girls expecting positive reactions from them. Instead, she was received by grim faces. Her expression suddenly matched theirs. "What's wrong?" Ara asked them.

"What is the date today?" inquired Hidayah.

"It's the 28th of May. Why do you ask?" Ara questioned.

The Jannah Jewels all gulped nervously.

"We must meet with the Sultan immediately then," Hidayah told her. "We don't have much time."

"Okay, let's get you all geared up, and then we will go pray. General Hassan will take you to the Sultan's pavilion after that," Ara said.

"Won't the Sultan realize we are girls when he hears our voices?" Iman questioned.

"That's a good point," Ara realized. "Maybe we can have General Hassan speak to him on your behalf. Let's not worry about that just yet and get ready first," she suggested.

She helped the Jewels layer up over their party dresses with pants, vests, long coats, and metal-netted armor suits. The girls quickly buttoned and laced up their gear.

"You will need to stuff these into your boots," Ara said handing scraps of fabric to each Jewel. "These will make you look taller and help you fit into your boots better."

The girls followed her instructions efficiently. Once they were completely dressed, they exchanged looks of playfulness with one another.

"It's like playing dress-up," said Iman with a smile.

"Except for the fact that we are going to war," Jaide clarified. The mood in the tent became heavy again.

"That's not making me feel better," Sara complained. "I don't have a good feeling about this. We have never done anything like this before. What if we get caught? I feel like we are playing with fire."

Iman stared at Jaide with irritation for upsetting Sara. "Sensei warned us of having to face many obstacles," she reminded Sara. "But remember what Master Runner taught us: *the only limitations you have are the ones you set for yourself*. I know Allah will send us help to get through this. Don't worry." She bent down to pick up a pointed steel helmet with a flat metal plate in the front to protect the nose. A red and white feather stuck out from the tip of the helmet's highest point. "Do we have to wear these? They are so heavy," Iman noted, trying to quickly change the subject.

"Yes," Ara answered. "They will keep your faces

hidden."

"How will I wear my eyeglasses?" Iman worriedly asked.

Ara shrugged her shoulders. "I presume you cannot then."

Iman let out a deep sigh. She removed her glasses and placed them into her satchel. Lifting the helmet carefully, she placed it gently over her *hijab* and set it nicely on her head.

"How do I look?" she asked the others.

"Like you are ready for battle!" Ara said beaming with pride.

Hidayah, Jaide, and Sara grabbed their helmets and did the same as Iman.

"Okay, are we all ready?" asked Ara.

Four feathered helmets nodded in agreement.

"Remember: outside this tent, I am Sir Ilyas." Ara put out her lantern and then poked her head out of the tent. She gestured the girls to follow her. They each snuck out carefully behind her.

Soldiers were beginning to come out of their

tents and crowd the military encampment as they washed up for the upcoming prayer with the water warming in the kettles above the campfires. The Jannah Jewels weaved through the men, keeping their gazes down and distance close to Ara. The air was filled with the echo of the call to prayer. They arrived to a large, open field decorated with endless rows of men lined up to pray.

"*Subhan Allah—Glory be to God!* Look at how many soldiers there are!" Jaide exclaimed.

"Shhh. Keep your voices low," Ara instructed. "We will stay in the back of the congregation to draw less attention to ourselves."

"Who will be leading the prayer?" Hidayah asked.

"The Sultan himself," answered Ara.

Hidayah looked around and noticed two soldiers who were shorter compared to the rest of their row.

They seem smaller-framed like us, she thought to herself. She tried to see their faces, but they were hidden behind their helmets just like the Jewels.

The *Fajr* prayer began, and the air rang with the deep, beautiful voice of the Sultan leading the prayer.

After the prayer ended, Hidayah looked back up in search of the two small soldiers. The taller of the two happened to look back. Through the narrow slits in the helmet, Hidayah recognized those two silver eyes: it was Jaffar.

7

Lost

Jaffar's eyes burned with exhaustion. He had spent the day in contemplation. After calling for help and rushing his father and sister to the hospital, he remained in deep prayer and thought.

This is not how things were supposed to be. Jaffar had spent most of his childhood trying to please his father. Nothing he did made his father happy. After his mother abruptly left home, Jaffar did everything he could to reconnect with Khan, as he was all he had left. In doing so, he had become someone he was not.

He had seen such dark sides of his father and sister lately. Why had Khan and Jasmin become like this? Jaffar did not want to be like them. He wanted to be like who his mother had named him after: Jaffar ibn Abi Talib, the Companion and cousin of the Prophet, peace and blessings be upon him.

"Dude, are you going to finish that?" Moe asked pointing at Jaffar's bowl of lentil soup.

Jaffar looked at his friend realizing where he was all of a sudden: in Moe's kitchen.

"Sorry. I'm not really hungry."

"Don't mind if I do then," Moe said as he slid Jaffar's bowl close to his side of the table.

Jaffar watched as Moe took loud, big slurps of the soup into his pudgy mouth, which had drips of soup hanging already from his first helping.

"How are you eating that? It's so cold and bland," Slim criticized with disgust.

"What did you say?" Moe looked up at Slim offensively.

Slim suddenly became still. "Uh, nothing! I love your mom's cooking!" he answered as he reluctantly took a sip of soup from his spoon.

"Give it a rest, guys," Jaffar interrupted. He placed his head between his hands and looked down at the round, wooden table. "I need to figure out what I'm going to do. I can't go home. And I feel like we should help the Jannah Jewels somehow. What do you guys think?"

"What? No way, Bro! We're too scared of your dad! You can hang here as long as you like, though, until your dad gets better," Moe told him. "We can be roommates," he suggested as he wiped his mouth on his sleeve covering it with brown residue from the thick soup.

"As tempting as that sounds, I'm going to have to pass," Jaffar said politely.

"How come?" Moe asked puzzled. He picked up the empty bowl and walked over to the stove to refill it.

Jaffar's head scrambled for a good excuse. "You have three sisters in the house. I wouldn't want to impose."

"You can always stay with me," Slim offered, his big eyes looking at Jaffar kindly. "I got no sisters, only little brothers."

"He might as well stay in a zoo then," Moe chuckled.

"Hey!" Slim yelled. "What is that supposed to mean?" Slim stood up, his chair making a loud screech against the tiled floor. "*You* belong in a zoo!"

The ground shook as Moe charged his heavy body towards Slim tackling him hard onto the floor. The two started wrestling and screaming names at one another.

Jaffar froze in disbelief not knowing what to do. He quickly put himself in the middle of them and pried them apart.

"Guys! Guys! Enough! We need to work together here. I need your help. I'm tired of acting like we are a bunch of bad guys. This is not us."

The room fell silent. Moe and Slim sat up but remained quiet.

"Are you guys with me or not?"

Moe and Slim diverted their glances away from Jaffar. Neither of them answered.

"I pray you guys will eventually come around," his voice carried a tone of disappointment.

He quietly stood up and walked out from the back door of the kitchen onto the busy streets of Fes.

What do I do now? Where should I go? Jaffar wondered. He never felt so lost in his life. All he knew was that he wanted to be better: a better kid, a better person, a better Muslim.

Uncle Idrees! Jaffar quickly thought of his beloved uncle, Khan's older brother. He began to run as fast as he could to his uncle's house.

He arrived there and was received warmly by his uncle and aunt. They were an older couple who never had children of their own. Jaffar always felt close to Uncle Idrees. He could talk to him about anything without ever feeling judged or criticized. His uncle seemed to just accept Jaffar for who he was and treated him like he was his own son.

Jaffar quickly relayed to Uncle Idrees and Aunt Nur everything that had just happened between his family and the Jannah Jewels.

"How are your father and Jasmin doing now?"

asked Aunt Nur.

The doctors said Jasmin has a hairline fracture in her arm and should be okay soon," told Jaffar. "As for Father…," his voice became faint as he held back his tears, "he has a serious concussion and is still unconscious."

"Oh God!" said Uncle Idrees. "I must go see him at once!"

"But he told you he never wants to see you again," Aunt Nur said hesitantly.

"We don't hold grudges, Noori," Uncle Idrees reminded her as he adjusted the rimless cap on his bald head. "We forgive others, so one day God will forgive us. He is my little brother. I have to go see him. Come with me, Jaffar."

Jaffar gazed at his uncle with uncertainty. "I can't, Uncle. Sorry."

"Jaffar! He is your father! You must be there for him in his time of need!" Uncle Idrees spoke firmly.

"I can't get over what Father did: he kidnapped the Jannah Jewels and that curly-haired boy!

Kidnapped! How could he do such an awful thing? His greed for power has taken him over!" Jaffar was furious. "If you want to go see him, so be it. I'm not going with you!" he shouted as he stormed out the door.

He ran and ran and ran. He did not know which way to go, but he kept running. He was frustrated, hurt and alone.

The call for the midday prayer rang from the city's numerous minarets. He approached a nearby mosque, made *wudhu*, and joined the congregation.

Oh God, forgive me for my sins. Oh God, guide me to You. Oh God, I need you now more than ever. Each time he bowed his head, another supplication poured out of his heart. He realized he was nobody without God by his side.

After the prayer, his eyes fell upon a quote by Jalal ad-Din Muhammad Rumi framed on the tiled wall of the mosque: "Yesterday I was clever, so I wanted to change the world. Today I am wise, so I am changing myself."

Jaffar felt a confirmation in his heart that God

had heard his prayers. *It's time to change for good*, he decided.

*   *   *   *

Jaffar knocked on the wooden door. His feet were sore from walking all this way. He was tired and hungry. He waited quietly as he heard quick footsteps approach the door.

"Who's there?" a voice called out from inside.

"It's Jaffar," his voice slightly cracked with hesitation.

Locks clicked open and a chain loosened. The door slid partially open. A face peeked out from behind, his curly hair seeping over his forehead.

"What do you want?"

Jaffar took a deep breath. "I need to talk to you. Please. I don't know where else to go," he spoke with desperation.

The door fully opened, and the tall, young boy curiously glared at Jaffar.

"Why me? I don't even know you."

Jaffar thought hard before he answered the

boy. "I want to help the Jannah Jewels just like you did. I won't be able to do that without your help." He reached his hand out to the boy.

The boy stared at Jaffar's hand and then back at his face, his expression composed and serious. He slowly brought his right hand forward and then locked his grip tight with Jaffar's.

"Tell me your name," said Jaffar.

"My name is Mus'ab. Tell me your plan."

8

A New Team

The Jannah Jewels looked up as a flock of birds circled the clear morning sky. Their screeches were loud and piercing.

"Those are hawks. It sounds as if they are trying to warn us of something," Iman whispered to the girls.

The field had become bustling with noise and traffic as the sea of soldiers began to disperse back to the encampment after the *Fajr* prayer.

"No one seems to even notice them," Jaide pointed out.

Hidayah did not pay much attention to them either. She was too busy keeping an eye on Jaffar and the other soldier, who were scanning the crowd and not moving from their places.

"This is the best time to move," Ara spoke to the girls. "Everyone is heading back to their tents, so we can easily head to General Hassan without being noticed.

"Sir Ilyas, I have to check something first," Hidayah spoke softly as to not be heard.

"What is it? There's no time to waste," said Ara.

Hidayah drew herself close to the other Jewels. "I think Jaffar is here."

The girls froze with shock.

Is he here for the artifact?" questioned Iman.

"No. It can't be," Jaide responded. "He tried to save Sara and me from his dad in Morocco, remember? Where is he? I'll go talk to him. I've been meaning to thank him for what he did anyway."

"You really think he's changed for good?" asked Iman.

"We only try to think the best of people, Iman," Hidayah reminded her. "Remember what Sensei

Elle said: *Allah is the Changer of Hearts. He guides who He wills."*

"Gentlemen, we must go now," Ara spoke in her deepest voice possible.

Hidayah moved in closer to her. "We think we've been followed here by those two smaller soldiers over there. We need to go see who they are."

Ara's face looked whiter in the morning light. "How do you know?" she asked. "You can't take the risk of being identified as girls."

"Then we need you to go check for us," Hidayah responded. The Jannah Jewels all glared at Ara through their helmets. "Please," Hidayah begged.

It was clear that Ara was uncomfortable with the idea. "Okay, if I must," she sighed and nervously walked up to the two lonesome soldiers. They seemed to become startled by her. The Jewels could see Ara questioning them but could not make out her words.

"Who is with Jaffar?" Sara wondered. "Could it be Jasmin?" The fear was apparent even through Sara's whispering.

"Why would he bring Jasmin with him?" asked Jaide. "Besides, Jasmin's not as tall as that guy." Jaide then looked closely and noticed Jaffar's companion carrying a black fabric drawstring bag on his back over his armor. Her eyes lit up when she saw something red sticking out from the bag's opening.

Jaide gasped. "My old skateboard! Could it be? It is! That's *Mus'ab* with Jaffar!" she shrieked forgetting to keep her voice feeble.

Both the soldiers and Ara suddenly turned to look at the Jewels. Mus'ab came running towards them clumsily, his limp more evident under the armor.

"*Salaam!* Oh mi gosh! Is it really you guys?" he asked in surprise.

"*Wa alaikum as salaam!* Mus'ab, what are you doing here?" Jaide asked completely astonished to see him.

"Man, I thought I would never see you guys again. Then, out of nowhere, Jaffar shows up and asks if I wanted to join him in helping you guys. I couldn't say no. You know me. I'm always up for an adventure!" Mus'ab said enthusiastically. Jaffar and Ara had walked over to the group now.

"*As salaamu alaikum*," Jaffar greeted the Jannah Jewels. "We didn't know how we'd find you guys amongst all these soldiers, but it seems God brought us right to you." His voice was calm and sincere.

"*Wa alaikum as salaam*," the Jewels replied together.

There was a long, awkward pause for some time. It was strange for Hidayah and the others to see Jaffar in this new light.

"Umm, Jaffar, we want to thank you for standing up to your dad for us," Jaide broke the silence. "You really saved us back there in Fes."

Jaffar looked down at his feet. "It was nothing," he mumbled.

Sara wanted to say something too, but she stopped herself. She still felt guilty for what she did to Khan.

"Gentlemen, I hate to break up the reunion here, but we really must go see General Hassan," Ara interrupted. "We mustn't keep him waiting."

"Yes, Sir Ilyas," Hidayah answered keeping Ara's identity hidden. "Come with us," she told the boys.

The Jannah Jewels along with Mus'ab and Jaffar followed Ara through the crowded field.

"Jaffar and Mus'ab being here will really help as they can speak to the Sultan instead of us," Hidayah told the group as they walked collectively behind Ara.

"The Sultan?" Mus'ab questioned. "As in Sultan Muhammad the Second?! Are we really going to meet him? Do you have any idea who he is or how amazing he is?!" Mus'ab could barely contain himself.

"Yes, we have some idea from what Iman's *Book of Knowledge* stated about him," Hidayah answered. "We think he can help us find the next artifact. However, if he hears our voices, he will know we are not males. There are no females allowed in the infantry."

"Wait. Then how does Sir Ilyas know who you are?" Jaffar questioned skeptically.

"General Hassan found us when we arrived here and took us to Sir Ilyas," answered Hidayah. "They both have kept our identities concealed, *Alhamdullilah*."

"Okay, but won't the Sultan realize Jaffar and I are too young to be here?" Mus'ab worried.

Ara slowed her footsteps. "Not necessarily. Military cadets start at age 14. Just act slightly older."

"I'm nowhere near 14, though!" Mus'ab spoke up.

"Stay silent then," Ara smirked and hurried ahead again.

"Do you know what the artifact is?" Jaffar asked the Jewels.

Hidayah took a moment to speak. "No," she replied. "Unfortunately, we had to leave in a rush, and I don't have my ancient map with me," she frowned behind her helmet remembering Sensei Elle being missing.

"Mus'ab and I checked my copy," Jaffar told them. "We think it's a necklace of some sort."

"Okay, that's good to know. It gives us something to start with," said Hidayah. "Where did you guys get all your gear from?"

"We saw on the map we were headed to Constantinople. We've been preparing for battle for the last month," answered Jaffar.

Suddenly, it occurred to Hidayah why Sensei Elle made them train so hard with Master Runner. She kept her thoughts to herself as she did not want to upset Sara again.

In broad daylight, the encampment was a spectacular sight to see, decorated with endless colorful tents. The Jannah Jewels and the boys were impressed with how regulated the arrangement of the numerous tents was.

"How did they bring all these tents here?" Jaide questioned. "This must have taken so much preparation and organization, no?"

"With the help of thousands of men, camels, horses, and oxen," Ara told them.

The military camp looked like a well-established system. They passed by tents of various sizes and colors, some with domed roofs, each with distinct functions: tents for provisions, others for equipment. The group saw cobblers at work repairing army shoes and boots. There were tents for laundry, cooking, for weaponry, and much more.

"It looks like a mini city," Sara noted.

"Yeah, it's as if they moved everything with them. So cool!" Mus'ab chimed in.

"We are entering the tents of the Janissaries, the strongest and best soldiers in the infantry," Ara informed the group. "Stick together now."

Keeping close proximity with one another, the new team weaved through the maze of tents, which increased in size as they continued walking. Hidayah noticed they were grouped by colors. From afar, she could see General Hassan standing and waiting in front of one of the larger tents.

"What's that on his arm?" asked Sara.

"It's a hawk!" exclaimed Iman. She quickly sped up to catch up with Ara. "Is General Hassan a falconer?" she asked her.

"Yes, he is," she answered with a smile. "Did you see the hawks flying above us at *Fajr* time? They belong to many of the falconers here. Falconry is a rich tradition in Ottoman heritage. On a military campaign like this, they help hunt for food with their powerful claws and keen eyesight. Isn't that a beautiful raptor he has?"

Iman grew excited as they neared the hawk. It was large and stocky with a hooked beak, strong legs, and sharp talons. It had a rich brown color with a white breast, a streaked belly, and a banded tail. As she grew closer, she saw its wings had a dark bar between its shoulder and wrist.

"*Glory be to God*, what a beauty!" Iman said as she approached it. The hawk stared hard at Iman. "*Salaam*, Beautiful," she greeted the bird.

"His name is Shuja'ah," General Hassan told her. "He's a very courageous bird, and the Sultan's favorite."

Iman gently stroked the hawk's feathered belly with her forefinger.

"Whoa! He's awesome! Can I pet him?" Mus'ab

asked as he walked up to them.

General Hassan glared at Mus'ab. His tall, broad built towered over him. "Awesome? What kind of word is that? And who are you anyway?" he questioned him.

Through his helmet, Mus'ab nervously looked up at the commander.

"I told you better to stay silent," Ara laughingly whispered to Mus'ab. His cheeks flushed with embarrassment.

"Sir, these are two more members of our team," Hidayah quickly intervened and told General Hassan. "This is Mus'ab, and this is Jaffar," she informed him as she pointed to each respectively. "Will you be able to take us to the Sultan now?"

"Yes, but the Emir is meeting with him at the moment," General Hassan informed them. "I am sure we will have to wait once we get to the Sultan's pavilion. Follow me and try not to talk or draw any attention to yourselves," he instructed, giving Mus'ab a stern look. "There will be many guards there." He walked Shuja'ah over to one of his men and placed him gently on the soldier's arm. The bird kept his gaze on Iman.

"This way," the commander then led the group onward.

They all followed General Hassan whose stride was like a tiger's causing his long hair to sway behind him. He led the group to some heavily-guarded, secluded grounds. Immediately, the kids felt as if they had stepped into a different world. It was a grand complex centered with an enormous imperial tent, its corners outlined with crimson flags blowing in the wind.

"Wow, it looks like a palace!" Jaide said leaning into Sara.

There were many sets of guards, each staring at the group as they approached them. As General Hassan passed by them, the guards stood up taller and stiffer greeting him loudly with *salaam* and lowering their gazes.

"He must be really important," Jaffar turned and whispered to the Jewels. They all nodded in agreement.

Hidayah realized how God had sent General Hassan right to them and had kept them protected thus far just like she had prayed. She quietly made another quick *du'a* in her heart asking God to continue protecting their team and grant them more openings on this mission.

The two guards in front of the imperial tent blocked the entrance with their spears as General Hassan approached them. "We apologize, Sir, but we have specific instructions from the Sultan not to let anyone in," said one of the guards.

General Hassan remained composed keeping his dark brown eyes focused on one of the guards. "Are they still in a meeting?" he asked.

"Yes, Sir," the guard answered.

"We will wait then," the commander said calmly. He walked up to Sir Ilyas. "Once the Sultan is ready to see them, I will walk them in, but you must return back. Do not talk to anyone," he told Sir Ilyas who nodded silently. General Hassan then signaled two guards to come forward. "Take Sir Ilyas back to his quarters once we enter the Sultan's pavilion."

The guards lowered their gaze affirmatively.

It seemed as if they waited outside the tent forever. The temperature had become warmer as the sun rose higher in the cloudless sky. The Jannah Jewels stood silently only exchanging looks of comfort at one another. No one knew what to expect or how the Sultan would receive them.

The flaps to the entrance of the great tent finally lifted, and an old man dressed in white long robes, with white hair and a stark white beard stepped out. He carried a staff in his hand and wore a large turban on his head. Immediately, General Hassan walked up to greet him.

"*As salaamu alaikum*, Emir Aaq."

The man looked up at General Hassan giving him a welcoming smile, the sides of his eyes forming wrinkles in his skin. "*Wa alaikum as salaam*." His bright eyes then fell upon the team of young soldiers quietly staring at him in wonderment behind their helmets. Pressing the staff to the ground with each step, he walked slowly up to the Jannah Jewels, Jaffar and Mus'ab.

89

"So, I see you all have finally come," he said in a gentle voice. "Peace be upon each of you. The Sultan and I have been waiting for you six. Welcome."

9

Openings

The new team was welcomed into the Sultan's tent like they were royalty. They scanned the walled palace in awe.

The tent walls consisted of rows of countless rectangular panels worked in a design of columns linked by arches, and majestic posts supported its high roof. The ornamentation was exquisite: a perfect combination of beauty and grandeur, a dwelling fit for a ruler. It was richly decorated with floral pattern designs. There were cloths hanging of vibrant colors embroidered in stitches of silk and metal threads as well as strings of lanterns dangling from above. The walls were thick but still thin enough to leak sunlight through them. The floor was lined with intricately weaved, plush carpets and rugs with rows of tall candle stands leading all the way to the opposite end of the tent, which was crowned with a large throne. There, sitting atop in all his glory, was Sultan Muhammad.

He was young and pale but strong looking with small, brown eyes and a pointy, sharp nose. He wore a dark red cap wrapped inside a large white turban that folded the top of his ears down. Layers of fabric covered his large body under a dark, red cloak and shawls, which rested perfectly on his wide shoulders.

The air felt cool inside the tent to the Jewels and smelled of incense. The only sound came from their armor clamoring against their bodies as they walked slowly behind Emir Aaq.

This must be a dream, Hidayah thought to herself. She could not believe where they had come.

The Sultan arose from his seat as they drew closer to him, keeping his expression serious. His presence seemed powerful, causing the girls to quickly lower their gazes out of respect for him.

Jaffar trailed behind at the back of the group, making quiet supplications to himself. He then quickly lined up with the others in front of the Sultan's throne. General Hassan followed and stood next to the Emir.

"Welcome," greeted the Sultan, his voice deep but inviting. "Emir Aaq tells me you all have traveled from very far to help our mission." He paused briefly. "We have been here for 52 days trying to enter Constantinople. How can you six possibly help us at this point?"

None of them spoke up.

"Oh, young ones, answer the Sultan," Emir Aaq told them.

The Jewels looked over at Jaffar and Mus'ab, both frozen like them. Jaffar, being the older of the two realized what he had to do. He then took a deep breath and sent prayers upon the Prophet Muhammad, which immediately brought a smile on the Sultan's face. Jaffar took a step forward.

"I begin with the name of Allah, the Most Gracious, the Most Merciful. Oh, great King, I was a person of ignorance: forgetting that I was a mere servant of Allah, and always trying to please the creation instead of the Creator. I let my desires overpower my heart, my anger rule my decisions, and my greed control my actions. But praise be to God, who has shown me where selfishness can take you: to one's demise. I realize now how wrong and alone I was without Allah. Mus'ab and I are honored to be here today with these Jannah Jewels to serve our Lord and only Him, for He is The Peace. We come to you over other leaders as you are known for being just. We are here to bring you hope and encouragement and glad tidings of the Prophet's promise being true. Surely, you are the wonderful leader who will conquer Constantinople, and if you let us, we would like to be part of your wonderful team," said Jaffar, who then quickly lowered his gaze.

Hidayah and the other Jewels' eyes were full of tears. They looked up at the Sultan whose beard was soaked with tears, and so was Emir Aaq's. Mus'ab placed his gloved hand on Jaffar's shoulder and gave him a look of acceptance. The grand room remained silent for some time.

"Glory be to Allah!" Emir Aaq finally spoke up wiping his tears. "*This* is what I have been telling you since you were a young child yourself, Ya Muhammad. You are chosen. May Allah continue to increase you."

The Sultan smiled humbly.

Emir Aaq then turned to the young team. "Do you know whose resting place is in these great lands?"

They all shook their heads.

"Outside this city's walls lies a close companion of the Prophet Muhammad, peace and blessings be upon him, named Khalid ibn Zayd, also known as Abu Ayub al-Ansari. He was the host of the Prophet when he first arrived to the city of Madinah from Makkah. The Prophet lived in Abu Ayub's home for over seven blessed months," the Emir told them.

The Jannah Jewels became overjoyed at hearing Emir Aaq say the word 'host.'

"Please tell us more," Jaffar requested.

"When this great companion, may God be pleased with him, was in his eighties, he came all the way from Madinah to try and bring Islam to these lands. He stuck with the army even in his old age, hoping to see the Prophet's predication come true about a victory in Constantinople. Unfortunately, he died in 674 AD of an illness but remained resilient not to leave these walls until his last breath. We must learn from his great example."

The Jannah Jewels and the boys listened wide-eyed in amazement.

"God is showering us with His blessings. We must come together and seek His help," the Emir raised his hands up in the air and prayed, "Oh God, You are the Host of All Hosts. Bring for us a great opening soon for Your sake, and honor this blessed city to host your beautiful religion and become a home for this wonderful leader as Abu Ayub hosted Your *Beloved* in his home. May the words of Your Prophet, the Elite One, be recognized through this Sultan's leadership making him an Opener for Your religion. May You shower Your Peace and blessings upon Your Messenger and all his companions, *Ameen*."

"*Ameen*," the gathering hummed together.

The Jannah Jewels all smiled at one another for the Emir had clarified more of Sensei's poem for them with his *du'a*. They gathered close to each other and squeezed each others' hands quietly with joy.

"I have declared today to be an official day of prayer and rest," Sultan Muhammad told the young team. "Please take the day to gather up your strength. I shall have my men take great care of you all. You need not worry about a thing. We will reconvene at *Tahajjud* time tonight, *in sha Allah*." He then looked over at General Hassan. "General, please make sure all their accommodations are taken care of and see where and how they can assist your Janissary troops tonight."

"Yes, Sir," replied General Hassan.

"*As salaamu alaikum*," the Sultan said to the team as he excused himself. He then slowly walked out with Emir Aaq and his guards.

*   *   *   *

General Hassan walked Jaffar and Mus'ab to

a large hosting tent. "The staff here will make sure everything is taken care of for you both. Please make yourselves comfortable. I will be back after the midday prayer to check up on you.

"*Jazak Allah khair*, may God reward you with goodness," the boys thanked him.

Before they separated, Jaide walked up to Mus'ab. "Hey, can you hand me your skateboard?" she asked him.

He gave her a questionable look. "Why? You want it back?"

Jaide shook her head. "No. No. I have a plan. Just hand it over in its carrier. I'll explain later," she told him.

Mus'ab hesitantly did as she asked. The boys then bid farewell to the Jewels for the time being and entered their tent.

As he led the girls away, General Hassan informed them that he was taking them back to Sir Ilyas. "You'll be safe there," he told them.

The Jannah Jewels felt at ease with that idea.

They followed the commander through the various regiments until they reached Ara's tent again. She was sitting outside boiling water in an iron kettle above a flame. She looked up at the girls pleasantly.

"*Alhamdullilah*, you all are back. I was just about to make some tea. Please, go have a seat in my tent. I will bring some cups inside for you," she welcomed the Jewels.

General Hassan left. The girls entered Ara's tent completely exhausted. They removed their helmets, boots and most of their armor and relaxed themselves against the numerous cushions on the floor.

"What's your plan with the skateboards?" Sara asked Jaide as she stretched her legs. Ara happened to walk in holding a pair of clay, mug-like vessels with hot tea steaming from them.

"Ara, we need your help," Jaide began speaking as she removed the two skateboards from their carriers. "These are wheeled boards we use for riding. I want to know if you can link them together with some type of iron chain or something."

"I will have to look at them carefully, but it should not be too hard," said Ara. "I will sneak them to the foundry tents and work on them privately. Here, have some tea for now. Then while you all get some rest, I will go see what I can do about these boards, *in sha Allah*," she said.

Hidayah, Jaide, Iman and Sara shared the soothing cups of Turkish tea, which helped calm their nerves. The girls then began to spread themselves out on the carpeted tent floor and quickly fell fast asleep.

Sara was running as fast as she could towards the wall. It was coming closer and closer. I must reach it. I must climb it, she told herself. She prepared to launch herself onto the wall at full speed pushing her feet hard up off the ground. As she propelled through the air, she was suddenly side-tackled to the ground by an armored figure charging at her. Her body pounded against the stiff earth, the impact taking everything out of Sara. She took some time to realize where she was and what had happened. She opened her eyes and hazily saw the sharp tip of an arrow locked in its bow pointed right at her. The helmeted face peered down at her, evil seeping out of her gray eyes. "You will pay for what you did!" she screamed at Sara, and released her arrow....

"Aaaaahhh!" Sara screamed waking up sweat-ridden.

The Jannah Jewels were all startled awake.

"Sara! What's the matter? Are you okay?" asked Hidayah frantically.

Sara tried to catch her breath as she stumbled to speak. "She's here! Jasmin is here!"

10

The Conquest

"Wait here," General Hassan instructed the Jannah Jewels and the boys. "The Sultan is about to address the army."

The waning moon shined bright above their heads in the last third of the night. The team was heavily armored with shields and bows and arrows standing anxiously behind Emir Aaq. As they peeked through the many bodies standing in front of them, they could see soldiers assembled in rows for acres with pointed helmets, swords, spears, and standards; their faces glowed in the moonlight.

Sultan Muhammad stood in the front line facing his men. He was dressed for battle, ready to lead his tremendous army.

"I know we will pass these walls with courage," he told his men, his voice echoed loudly through the air. "But remember: you cannot achieve glory without faith. Allah is Great and by His will, together we will be able to pray *Dhuhr* on the other side of the wall in the Church of Hagia Sofia." He drew his sword from its casing and lifted it to the sky. "Allah is Great!" he shouted.

"Allah is Great!" the assembly of soldiers shouted back.

The intense wave of energy penetrated through the air. The Jannah Jewels' hearts raced with anticipation. They had never witnessed an event such as this before.

The Sultan instructed his army to spend the rest of the night in worship asking Allah for His help.

Hidayah, Iman, Jaide and Sara sat with Ara after offering prayers, doing *dhikr* of Allah, each tense and weary of what was yet to come. They kept their eyes alert, for Jasmin could be anywhere.

Sara wished she was back home, safely riding

her bike down her neighborhood street, playing tag with her friends. She did not want to be here. She did not want to face Jasmin.

"What's wrong?" Jaide asked her. "You okay?"

Sara took heavy breaths behind her helmet, her eyes big with fear. "I can't do this, Jaide. I don't know why Sensei chose us for this. What if we don't make it home? What if that's why your watch stopped working: because there's no going back?"

"We will stick together, Sara," Jaide consoled her. "This is one of the main reasons why I asked Ara to link the skateboards. We are a team, and we will get through this together *in sha Allah*."

Hidayah leaned into her friends. "Sara, if we do cross paths with Jasmin again, we have Jaffar and Mus'ab to help us this time. Plus, never forget that Allah is on our side."

"It's time," Ara told them.

"Aren't you scared?" Sara turned and asked her.

"No," she answered calmly. "We believe in what the Prophet, peace be upon him, promised: Islam coming to these very lands. We have been chosen to fulfill that promise. Each day, you need to be better than you were the prior day, and there is no better day than today to do just that."

Recognize the one behind the fire, for courage you will acquire. For the first time in one month, Sara's heart felt at ease, yet strong. She realized how much Ara's words echoed those of her mother and Sensei. She silently thanked Allah for bringing such great women into her life.

"Thank you," Sara whispered as she squeezed Ara's hand. "You have inspired me in more ways than you will ever know."

Ara squeezed Sara's hand in return and smiled warmly.

"*Bismillah,*" she told the girls as she stood up.

"In the name of God," they repeated, standing up after her.

They followed Ara through the crowd to their posting where General Hassan was waiting. He looked fearless and brave in his full armor. For the first time, his serious disposition did not greet the girls. When he saw the group coming, he welcomed them with a friendly smile.

"May Allah's Peace be upon each of you," he greeted them. "Are you all ready?"

"Yes, Sir!" the Jannah Jewels with Jaffar and Mus'ab answered firmly.

General Hassan smiled bigger. "*Alhamdullilah.* Today will be the day, *in sha Allah.* You will charge towards the wall with the cavalry. Keep yourself protected from the Byzantines' weapon of Greek fire as you near the wall. We must stick together and stick to the plan. If we do get separated, remember, I will meet you at the top of the flag tower *in sha Allah.*"

The six of them nodded confidently. General Hassan then led them through the massive army dressed in red under their armor, each member taking his position. Endless red flags waved high in the air.

The sun shined bright full of hope. Iman placed her hand over her eyes to shield them from the sunlight. She missed her glasses that automatically tinted from the solar rays.

As they continued walking, she looked over at Sara, who was valiant now, keeping her focus on the mission and not wandering her attention in search of Jasmin. Seeing Sara strong made Iman feel greatly secure at that moment.

They reached the cannon-firers first. The Jannah Jewels were full of awe. There were so many cannons, and in the center of them all stood Ara's giant bronze cannon.

"This is my stop," Ara told the Jewels.

They stared at her quiet and cheerless.

"You all have inspired me in ways you will never know," she said. "May Allah make you great standard-bearers of our *Ummah*. I love you all for His sake," her eyes glittered with faint tears.

The Jannah Jewels' hearts ached and grew heavy. They remained silent and strong for Ara had given them so much courage. They gestured good-bye and continued behind General Hassan to the frontlines and quickly positioned themselves with the cavalry.

Iman and Hidayah approached a tall Arabian horse. It was finely chiseled with a concave profile, its neck arched and tail high. Iman rubbed its soft brown coat and greeted it with a *salaam*. The horse blinked his large eyes in return. Iman climbed on first, then Hidayah behind her. They were surrounded by fierce horsemen all around.

"You going to be okay without your glasses?" Hidayah asked Iman leaning into her from the back.

"Yes, *in sha Allah*," she answered. "Allah is *Al-Musawwir*, the Fashioner. I told you guys He has designed the eyes in such a distinct way. My eyes have adjusted over the last day without my glasses."

Reassured, Hidayah turned back to take one last look at Ara. Over the heads of the horsemen, she could see Ara standing tall and ready with a large, long torch in her hand next to her massive cannon.

Meanwhile, Jaide and the others situated themselves right next to Iman and Hidayah's horse. Jaide looked at Mus'ab steadfast. "You make sure you steer your board in the same direction as mine," she told him firmly.

Mus'ab remained unruffled. "I'm with you," he reassured her.

Jaide then looked at Sara and Jaffar. "You both must keep yourselves and the boards balanced. It's like we will be surfing a huge wave. Listen for my orders, Sara. And Jaffar, you do what she does."

"*Ya Fattah*, open the way for us," Jaffar prayed out loud, no quiver in his voice.

"And open this city and our hearts to goodness," Sara added.

"*Ameen*," the team hummed.

They each climbed onto their boards: Jaide and Sara on the electric, Mus'ab and Jaffar on the back one. They looked up and saw Sultan Muhammad perched high up on his horse with General Hassan and the other standard-bearing riders circled around him. They were waiting for the signal; they were waiting for the great blast.

Everyone stared hard at the towering wall ahead. Drums pounded in the distance, but the Jannah Jewels' could not hear them over their own heartbeats. All was still with patience, and then—the air exploded, and the ground shook beneath their feet.

A section of the wall was bombarded from underneath. It immediately crumbled right in front of the team's eyes.

Not a second later, the Sultan screamed, "Fire the cannon!" A harsh, piercing blast came from behind them. A giant metal ball encircled in a trail of dark smoke flew overhead smashing hard against the weakened wall sending chunks of concrete flying. "Attack!" the Sultan ordered his people.

The cavalry took off with great force, the earth quaking beneath from its might. Heads low and bodies bent, the skateboarders kept their speed within the stampede through the large clouds of rising dust. Mus'ab moved in unison with Jaide's swift steering. They rapidly charged towards the wall determined and fearless. Hidayah, Iman, Jaide, Sara, Mus'ab and Jaffar felt alive and exhilarated from the impact of the wind hitting them.

They were quickly faced with the defending army. Arrows, some ablaze, came at them like a swarm of flies.

"Now!" screamed Jaide.

Sara raised her shield and lifted it above their heads like an iron umbrella. Jaffar did the same with his. As they weaved through the haze, arrows bounced off their shields making loud tapping sounds.

"Hidayah, be my eyes!" Iman shouted. Hidayah lifted her bow and started firing arrows at who ever tried blocking their way. She shot to the right, to the left, to the front, to the sky clearing their path like wildfire. Iman thundered forward keeping her focus on General Hassan, making sure she did not lose sight of the blazing commander.

As they drew near, Jaide saw the opposite infantry racing towards the Ottoman army. She knew just how they were going to maneuver through the Byzantine ground troops. "Squat down!" she ordered her wheeled riders.

Sara lowered herself maintaining her balance at the back of the electric skateboard. Jaffar followed suit. With her sword in her right hand and her shield

in her left, Sara guarded the right side. She whacked at the calves of the charging army buckling enemies to the ground, while Jaffar intercepted the ones to the left. Soldiers were falling all around continuously as the air was lit with fire and smoke. Yells were coming from all corners.

As they sliced through the blur of the black fog, the collapsing structure of the great wall came into sight. The riders quickly disbanded following General Hassan's example. Iman and Hidayah dismounted their horse and started warding off the enemy: Hidayah shooting arrows one-by-one, Iman using her sword.

"Jump off!" screamed Jaide, causing Sara, Mus'ab and Jaffar to leap off the moving boards. She then brought the chained boards to a halt and quickly stowed them away onto her back. She withdrew her sword and began fighting off the opposing army.

"Look out!" General Hassan warned his troops as a thick liquid rained down from the top of the tower. "It's Greek fire! This way!" General Hassan instructed all his men. The six young fighters ran behind their commander resiliently repelling any attackers and avoiding the lethal liquid. "We need to get our flag up to the tower!" he told them waving his sword frantically through the air with one hand and holding the red flag rolled tightly around a tall pole in the other.

"We'll help you, Sir!" Jaffar volunteered. He grabbed Mus'ab's hand, and together they cleared a path for General Hassan to reach the tower stairs. They zoomed up the stone staircase, protecting General Hassan from the front while he made sure no one attacked them from the back.

The Jannah Jewels ran after the boys but before they could reach the stairs, another bombardment instantly brought the staircase to shambles.

Mus'ab turned and looked down from the top. "Jewels!" he screamed.

The Jewels were tossed back from the great blow. They landed hard on the ground, gasping and wheezing for clean air. They waved their hands to clear the cloud of grainy smoke from their faces.

Hidayah looked up and saw Mus'ab standing a

great distance above them. "Go, Mus'ab, go!" she cried out through the gray fog.

The boys, not knowing what else to do, dashed after General Hassan and warded off the tower guards.

The Jannah Jewels struggled to get back on their feet amidst the chaos and wreckage. They quickly recollected themselves.

"What do we do now?" Jaide asked.

"*Climb high, climb fast, for there will be a great blast.* Parkour," Sara told the girls. The Jewels glared at the sky-scraping wall in front of them.

My Lord, You are the Most High. Raise us to new heights, Hidayah prayed in her heart. "I have an idea," she told the others. "Follow me." She took her shield and wore it on her back. She then darted super fast towards the crumbled staircase. She launched herself at the pile of broken rocks and began to climb, leap and bounce over the rubble.

"Wow, it looks just like the Terra Nova boulders back in Vancouver," said Sara, and she zoomed towards the rocks picking up great speed and climbed up the stone pile after Hidayah. Jaide then did the same. Iman hesitated slightly as her fear of heights had not fully cured.

Don't think. Just do, she told herself. She took a deep breath and called upon God for help as she forced her fears aside.

Climbing the rocks was much harder for the Jewels this time around with heavy armor and gear on their backs. To add to the difficulty, arrows were flying at them from all around bouncing off their shields and armor.

"Don't look down! Hurry!" Hidayah ordered.

All four Jewels sped up their climb and finally reached the top of the wall. They all took a moment to take in the battle scene below. It was complete mayhem.

"Get them!" a voice shouted nearby.

"Jaide! The skateboards!" Hidayah screamed.

Jaide yanked the boards from her back, and the Jewels immediately jumped on. "Iman, do as Sara does and keep your weight even with board.

Hidayah, shoot anyone who comes in our way," she instructed.

Like a torpedo, they zipped through the mob rushing towards the flag post. As Jaide dodged bodies and ruins, Sara and Iman used their swords to fight off any attackers. Hidayah released arrows one after another.

"Look! There they are!" Sara hollered at the sight of Mus'ab and Jaffar, who were whipping their swords blocking off the guards as General Hassan was trying to remove the Byzantine flag from the battlement. Hidayah aimed and began firing in their direction, the guards dropping like flies.

"We must help them!" Sara screamed. They jumped off their boards and rushed towards the boys. With their backs facing General Hassan, the six young soldiers formed a crescent-shaped human shield around him as he planted the Ottoman flag into its new post.

They used their shields and their swords to protect themselves as arrows flew at them non-stop.

A terrible cry came from behind them, one of

extreme pain. Hidayah turned back and saw General Hassan struggling and weak. Despite their efforts, he had been hit and badly wounded.

"Noooo!" Hidayah screamed.

The battle was over. The Prophet's prediction was fulfilled. The Ottoman red standard had been raised over Constantinople. General Hassan had returned to His Lord.

11

Returning Home

To God we belong and to Him we return.

The air had suddenly become still. The Jewels and the boys prayed for General Hassan. The morning sun was hovering over them, but they felt as if light had left them. The six of them kneeled and cried as their commander lay still.

"Why couldn't we save him?" Jaide weeped.

"Because we can't change history," Iman reminded them wiping her wet cheeks.

The children sat in silence for a long time blocking out all the mingled outpourings of jubilation and mourning around them. They were numb to the triumph that had just occurred. As the people celebrated the win, they grieved their loss.

A group of red-garbed members of the Sultan's service with tall headgear approached the pain-stricken circle.

"The Sultan has requested you six to join him at the gates," one of them informed them. "You may go. We will take care of the commander."

The six gathered their things and reluctantly stood up, their bodies covered in cuts and armor stained with dried blood. They did not feel any physical pain, though. Their hearts hurt more. They dragged their feet away from General Hassan's resting place.

*   *   *   *

The Jannah Jewels and the boys marched alongside the great procession through the grand gates of the first outer wall, red flags and standards raised high. The inner wall was some 20 meters away, its doors swung open as the Sultan neared it.

The great city was lit by the sun with pink and white, radiating and iridescent. The air was cool and clear of pollution from the battle. It was dotted with hills covered in white, magnificent structures, domed buildings, and beautiful green landscapes. Hidayah could not help but tear up in gratefulness. *"Alhamdullilah wa shukar Allah,"* she whispered to herself. No other words could describe her contentment at that moment. She looked back and could only see an endless sea of Muslims following behind them.

They approached the Church of Hagia Sofia, where many of the city's settlers had gone for refuge from the battle. The Sultan entered humbly smiling at the congregation of Christians who became timid in his presence.

"You need not worry," he told them. "You are a part of us now.

The people slowly raised their eyes towards their new leader.

"You are free to live according to your own faith," he reassured them.

The congregation rejoiced at his words cheering with joy and relief.

Sultan Muhammad walked back to Emir Aaq

who was smiling at the entrance of Hagia Sofia with satisfaction. The Jewels watched from behind the crowd as the Sultan reached into his armor belt and pulled out a *tasbih*. He whispered something to the Emir who then brought it over to the team.

"This belonged to the Sultan's late father. He wants you to have it."

The ancient artifact! the Jewels all simultaneously realized.

Jaffar reached his hand out as the Emir placed the *tasbih* into his palm.

At that moment, the call to prayer was made for the first time in Constantinople, and the Muslims prayed together in the new city. Afterwards, the team reconvened outside at the steps of the newly converted mosque.

"I think we should head back now," Hidayah told her team members who quietly agreed.

The group marched back out of the city's tall wooden gates. The aftermath of the battle was haunting outside the walls. For a long time they walked silently through the ruins until they reached the encampment field, which only had workers and maintainers left in it. The team searched for some food and an open space to catch their breaths. All they found were some chunks of hard bread near the food tent. They removed their helmets and armor and sat down to finally eat.

"For the first time, I didn't even have time to think about food!" said Jaide. "Now I realize how famished I am!" She grabbed a stale roll from a basket.

Jaffar slid off the Sultan's *tasbih* from his wrist. "So, it wasn't a necklace," he noted as he dangled it in the air, the sunlight making colorful prisms within its crystal beads.

"Can I see it?" asked Sara. She examined the string of beads carefully, taking in its intricate, yet simple design. "It's so beautiful," she said.

Iman leaned in to get a closer look. "It sure is," she agreed.

QAA! QAA!

The sudden screech startled the gang. Iman looked up to see Shuja'ah circling above them.

"He's warning us of trouble!" Iman shouted. "We must get out of here! Now!"

"But we don't even know where our tree to go home is," Jaide stated worriedly.

QAA! QAA!

"He will show us the way. Let's go!" said Iman.

They quickly gathered their belongings and began to run as fast as they could after Shuja'ah. They cut through the maze of tents trying not to lose sight of the fast-flying hawk.

Sara felt a moment of déjà vu. The scene was too familiar: her running for her life and being chased. She turned back and looked to see a horse rider charging towards them from a distance.

"Someone's coming after us!" she screamed as she lagged behind. "Run faster!"

The six of them picked up speed and ran even faster. However, they could not outrun the speed of the galloping rider, who was rapidly honing in on them.

The nightmare was not ending. Sara could not

wake up. This was all too real all of a sudden. She could feel her feet being lifted off the ground. She was being yanked upwards.

"Ahhhh!" she screamed as she was roughly tossed onto the back of the moving horse. Face down, she was teetering on her belly trying hard not to fall off. "Help me!"

"Sara!" screamed Jaide. She yanked out her skateboard and hopped on, but it was no use. "Noooooo! It's not starting! The battery's dead!"

"Oh no! What do we do?" screamed Hidayah. "She's getting away!"

Jaffar and Mus'ab continued to run after the lone rider, but they could not catch up by foot.

Iman did not waste another second. "Shuja'ah! Save Sara!" she commanded the hawk hovering above them.

Shuja'ah flapped his wings and soared through the air. He dived down like lightening and clenched the rider's *hijab* with his talons. Frightened, she released the reigns to fight off the bird's sharp claws. The horse continued to gallop into the forth-coming

forest.

"Let me go!" the rider screamed as Shuja'ah yanked at her head. The rider waved her arms frantically to swat the bird away, only to become completely disorientated.

"Aaahh!" she shrieked losing her balance and toppling off the moving horse. She hit the grass with extreme force. "My arm!" she cried.

Sara held on with all her might. She reached forward with all her strength and pulled the reigns back hard. The horse immediately began to slow down. She waited until he fully stopped and then carefully slid off. She then quickly ran back.

There was no trace of Sara's snatcher anywhere. It was as if she had vanished into thin air.

Hidayah and the others finally came running through the trees. Shuja'ah was resting on Iman's arm.

"Sara! Are you okay?" Jaide asked catching her breath.

"Yes, I'm okay, but the artifact...it was stolen

from me—by Jasmin!"

Jaffar's face became white. "What?! That was her?!" he asked in shock.

Sara nodded. "She could not have gotten that far. She fell off the horse and sounded like she was really hurt."

"We have to find her!" Jaffar shouted. "Let's split up."

The six of them searched the surrounding forest, while Shuja'ah scanned from above. There was no sign of her.

"She must have travelled back to Fes," Jaffar speculated as the group gathered back together. "I'll deal with her when I get back. Let's go, Mus'ab," he said.

"Wait. How can we go back without the artifact?" Hidayah worried.

Sara began to cry. "What are we going to do?" she asked fretfully.

Hidayah took a deep sigh. "Well, for starters, we definitely can't stay here," she stated.

"And what will we tell Sensei?" cried Sara.

"I don't know," answered Hidayah solemnly. "This has never happened before."

"Don't worry," said Mus'ab. "Jaffar and I will go back and get the artifact from Jasmin," he reassured the Jewels. "Jaide, hold on to my skateboard 'til next time," he told her. Jaide agreed.

The disheartened team separated in the hopes to meet again soon.

Shuja'ah guided the Jewels to their original Eastern plane tree. The Anatolian sun peeked through the canopy of the tall trees. The forest was cooler under the shade of the centennials.

Iman nuzzled her nose against Shuja'ah's beak. "General Hassan was right: you *are* a very courageous bird," she whispered. "We will miss you and him very much."

Sara then stroked his soft white belly with her fingers. "Thank you for saving me," she told the hawk.

He spread his mighty wings wide and lifted

himself up through the trees and high up in the air.

"Peace!" Iman bid farewell to him.

"Ready?" Hidayah asked standing next to the wide trunk of the enormous tree, her voice thick and wavering.

Iman, Jaide and Sara took deep breaths. "Ready," they all responded.

The Jannah Jewels pushed the centennial tree as hard as they could and down, down, down they went sliding through the tunnel.

When they reached the bottom, they locked hands and recited in unison, *"Bismillah hir Rahman nir Raheem!"*

There was a great whirring sound. They opened their eyes to the warmth of their favorite misty maple tree. The air smelled sweet and welcoming. The lanterns were dimly lit and all was quiet.

They heard subtle footsteps coming towards them through one of the underground tunnels. The girls each secretly hoped their Sensei had safely returned.

A lean shadow appeared before them. "*As salaamu alaikum,*" a soft, familiar voice greeted the Jewels.

"Sensei!" they all screamed and ran to her with open arms. They wrapped themselves around her and hugged her tightly.

"I missed you all too," she told them warmly, returning their hugs. As the girls released her one-by-one, Sensei saw their eyes sparkle with tears.

"What troubles you all so? Tell me. How was your mission, Hidayah?" she asked sincerely.

Hidayah swallowed hard, tears still flowing from her eyes. "Sensei, we don't know how to tell you this…but…the ancient artifact…was…stolen."

To be continued…

Don't miss the next Jannah Jewels book!

Will the Jannah Jewels be able to retrieve the stolen artifact in time? Will Jaffar and Mus'ab find Jasmin back in Morocco? Will Khan's memory come back to him? Will the new team be reunited again for another mission?

Find out in the next exciting quest of the Jannah Jewels as they time travel to America.

Find out more about the eighth book by visiting our website at
www.JannahJewels.com

Glossary

As salaamu alaikum: Muslims greet each other with this prayer in Arabic meaning 'Peace be upon you'

Wa alaikum as salaam: reply in Arabic meaning 'and Peace be upon you'

Jazak Allah khair: a prayer in Arabic meaning 'May God reward you with goodness'

In sha Allah: Arabic for 'God-willing'

hijab: head-covering

Bismillah: Arabic for 'with the name of Allah'

Masha Allah: Arabic for 'Allah has willed it thus'

salaam: Arabic word for 'peace'

wudhu: ablution

Holy Qu'ran: sacred scripture of Islam

dhikr: remembrance of God

Fajr: the first prayer of the day at dawn

du'a: supplication

Surah Yaseen: the 36th chapter of the *Holy Qur'an*

Ameen: same as 'Amen,' it is the Arabic word to close a supplication

*God suffices us, and what a great Guardian is He. (Surah 'Aali 'Imran 3:173)

Bismillah hir Rahman nir Raheem: Arabic for 'in the name of God, The Most Gracious, The Most Merciful'

Tahajjud: the frame of time within the last third of the night

Qibla: Arabic word for 'direction' that a Muslim faces to pray

Peace is the word from the Merciful Lord. (Surah Yaseen 36:58)

Sultan: a title for a Muslim ruler

Alhamdullilah: Arabic for 'All praise is for Allah'

Dhuhr: the second prayer of the day

Ummah: Arabic for 'community'

Ya Fattah: Arabic for addressing God by His name 'The Opener'

To God we belong and to Him we return. (Surah al-Baqarah 2:156)

Shukar Allah: Arabic for 'thanks to God'

tasbih: a string of beads tied together to help keep count of one's supplications

To find out more about our other books,

go to:

www.JannahJewels.com

94206402R00085

Made in the USA
Columbia, SC
29 April 2018